THE LITTLE DICTIONARY
OF FASHION

THE LITTLE DICTIONARY OF FASHION

Christian Dior

A guide to dress sense for every woman

Abrams, New York

Introduction

Much has been written about Fashion, in all its aspects, but I do not think any *couturier* has ever before attempted to compile a dictionary on the subject.

Of course, it would take volumes to cover the entire field of Fashion, but I have compiled a book that I think is neither too long, so that it becomes tedious, nor too short so that it seems insufficient, and I have called it my *Little Dictionary of Fashion*.

I think it should be of great practical use to the women of today.

Many people dismiss *haute couture* as being something that is only for those who are very wealthy.

But it is possible for a woman to be elegant without spending very much money on her clothes, if she follows the basic rules of Fashion and is careful to choose the clothes that suit her personality.

Simplicity, good taste, and grooming are the three fundamentals of good dressing and these do not cost money.

First, you must study yourself. Learn to know what suits you and what does not. And study your own needs. Find the colors that flatter you and emphasize your looks. Avoid the colors that do nothing for you.

Choose clothes that are simple in line and pay great attention to their *fit*.

And above all—*care* for your clothes. You cannot be well groomed if your clothes are not well cared for.

tian dior

Accent

An accent is that little personal touch which makes a dress designed by a couturier your own dress. It is of great importance.

... Accent, for lovely hands and a slender wrist ... this many stranded necklace of anthracite beads is used with originality as a bracelet wound round and round the arm.

The accent must always have the touch of your personality ... The place you put a clip ... The way you tie a bow ... How you fold your scarf ... The color you choose for your flower ...

With your personal feeling no one can do it better than you ... But, be careful, one accent is enough. And if you choose a color accent, select it with great care—and remember that except in the hands of an expert two colors in one outfit is enough.

Accessories

They are so important to the well-dressed woman. The less you can afford for your frocks, the more care you must take with your accessories. With one frock and different accessories you can always be well turned out. But be always careful if you cannot have a complete set for each different color.

You must choose a color that will match many clothes in your wardrobe.

Unless you have a lot of money it is wiser to choose black, navy, or brown for your accessories rather than a bright red or green.

It is a question of care and taste.

Don't buy much but make sure that what you buy is good.

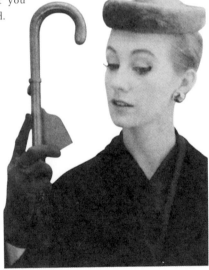

... Accessories are very important. Here an emerald green hat highlights a black suit. The leather-handled umbrella is from the Dior Boutique.

A

Adaptation

Be very careful of adapting any frock—or suit for that matter! When a frock has been created with much thought and care it is always very difficult to change the design without ruining it. It is always better if you can find another frock that is more convenient for you.

Any change is always an event—and you never know quite what will happen!

Afternoon Frock

There is little difference in design between a day frock and an afternoon frock—but the material is usually a little richer.

Of course you can wear a suit in the afternoon, too, but for later afternoon nothing is more useful than a frock which may be worn for cocktails or for dinner as well.

Black is the best color for it—in any material. If you can have only one afternoon frock I should always advise you to have it black.

And the most useful design is a dress with a décolleté—and a bolero or spencer. Any sort of material is good—from wool to lace. Any sort of bodice, and any kind of skirt—slim or full, it depends on your figure and the kind of life you lead.

... Age. Simple and elegant, this charming suit in brown wool is ideal for the "older woman." Dior accents it with a tiny hat in vivid cerise.

Age

As far as fashion is concerned there are only two ages—girlhood and womanhood.

(There are also grandmothers—but it is only necessary to dress as a grandmother if you have a certain kind of figure and lead a certain kind of life.) You can dress to suit yourself—and therefore your age—

A

but this does not mean that you have to wear clothes that make you look old.

There is a slight difference in a woman's way of dressing before and after marriage, too. I would not advise anyone to wear big jewels and expensive furs before marriage.

Aprons

By "apron" I do not mean the very necessary and very useful apron that you wear for your housework. In couture language, an "apron" is a piece of floating material which may change entirely the look of your skirt and give to it greater interest.

If your hips are not perfect and you wish to wear a slim frock, an apron put on the side or at the front or the back may help you very much to carry it off.

Armholes

In dressmaking the armhole is a very important part of a garment. If the sleeve sits badly the whole design is ruined; and if a frock doesn't fit perfectly the fault is very often found at the armhole.

The type of armhole is a matter of choice. But remember that too deep an armhole is very fattening.

Ball Gown

... Ball gown. Dior chooses rich satin for his dramatic black and white long evening dress and finishes the single ribbon band on the skirt with a large bow. The black and white theme is continued in necklace and ear-rings, which are of jet and brilliants.

A ball gown is your dream, and it must make you a dream ... I think it is just as necessary in a woman's wardrobe as a suit. And it is wonderful for morale ...

Wearing a beautiful ball gown you become a real woman ... all femininity and daintiness and sweetness.

You can choose almost any material—the richer the better—chiffon, satin, brocade, silks; and organdy and cotton for the younger set.

And any style—although I think full-skirted frocks look very romantic; and unless you are a little on the thin side, a strapless bodice is nice.

With a suit and a ball gown you can make a tour of the world and be well dressed for almost any occasion.

Belts

To wear a belt is the most wonderful way to emphasize your waist. Except for sports clothes or beach clothes, belts generally should be classic and in leather—although nice belts may be made in material to match your frock, too. And in a more dressy way, the draped belt (which you call sash) may be very elegant if you have a small waist.

Always be careful when you choose a belt to have it shaped to give you a longer and plunging line at the back. Whether you choose a wide or a narrow belt depends upon the style of frock or coat you are going to wear it with, but if you are short-waisted you should avoid wide belts.

Black

The most popular and the most convenient and the most elegant of all colors. And I say color on purpose, because black may be sometimes just as striking as a color.

It is the most slimming of all colors and, unless you have a bad complexion, it is one of the most flattering.

You can wear black at any time. You can wear it at any age. You may wear it for almost any occasion. A "little black frock" is essential to a woman's wardrobe.

I could write a book about black …

Blouses

Today blouses are not worn quite as much as they used to be and I think it is a pity.

Of course, many suits can be worn without a blouse, but I think it is very nice when it is warm enough for you to take off your jacket and show a pretty blouse.

And with some suits, especially if they have a skirt that is rather full, you can wear an embroidered blouse or one made in lace, velvet, or satin—then you can be well dressed for the evening as well as the daytime!

Blue

Among all the colors, navy blue is the only one which can ever compete with black, it has all the same qualities.

Pale blue is one of the prettiest colors, and if you have blue eyes no color is more becoming. Be careful when you are selecting a blue to see it both in daylight and electric light, because it changes very much.

Bodices

This is the most important part of any garment. It is near your face and has to make a nice frame for it.

Most of the interest in a dress is centered in the bodice and the cut of it is the keynote of the whole frock. The skirt is designed to balance the bodice. In the bodice a great amount of camouflage can take place. Those of you who are a little small about the bust can wear something a little fancy—perhaps some tucking or an elaborate collar.

And big sleeves—they will give you balance where they would look too heavy on the plump figure.

Buttons and a bow give interest to this pretty bodice.

A boat-shaped neckline if you are long waisted.

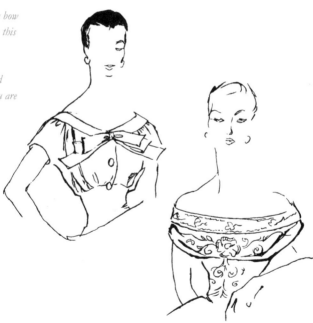

Simplicity for the perfect figure, accentuated by a large bow.

Fluted bodice flattering to the slender girl.

A draped bodice is good for you, too … flowing lines from the shoulder seams.

The person who is short waisted needs to have long lines in the bodice—V necks, seams running from the shoulder to the waist and small buttons not large ones.

The long-waisted person is lucky—length from shoulder to waist is very graceful. And she should concentrate on making her waist look as tiny as possible. A little width on the shoulders, yokes and boat-shaped necklines will all do this for you.

The people who are not-so-slim about the bust also need to make their waist the focal point as long as it is a small waist. They should choose bodices with soft, flowing lines, a little drapery perhaps; but nothing fussy. Deep V-necks, especially with a contrasting collar are good for you, also asymmetrical lines.

When your figure is perfect, the simpler the bodice the better. It may be intricately cut to give you a "sculptured" look, but to the casual glance it will look simple.

Boleros

Boleros are a very convenient way to change the look of a dress. They can be in the same material as the dress or in contrasting material or color.

They are especially good for long-waisted people.

A bolero worn with a décolleté dress gives it a town look. An embroidered or velvet bolero gives a simple frock a dressy look.

A colored bolero gives a black frock a touch of brilliance or a spring touch if you wish it.

Lastly, a fur bolero is a very convenient and elegant way to wear furs. If you get cold it will keep you warm as well as looking nice. Being near the face, a bolero is very important for glamorizing.

Boning

With the simplification of life and of fashion, the boning of dresses has come into use—and this does away with the heavy corsets our grandmothers wore.

When you wear a strapless dress, boning is absolutely essential.

Bows

The most natural ornament of a dress because they are a natural way of closing and tying material. I love bows to close a décolleté, trim a hat, or to fasten a belt. I like them big, small, or enormous, in any way and in any material.

But, one word of warning—they must be used with discretion and placed with care.

A narrow black bow trims the waistline of this short dinner dress in white grosgrain.

Brocade

The richest of all materials, brocade has to be used with great discrimination because, being so rich, it may not look young. That is why I advise you to use it for short evening dresses, full or narrow skirted, or for suits.

For long evening dresses, brocade should be used only for great ceremonies with a certain official character. The Coronation was a typical occasion for brocade. Its richness and luxuriousness did justice to the dignity of the event.

Brown

Brown is a very nice dark color, especially nice for suits and coats. And in silk it is also very charming for frocks and suits to wear with fur coats.

Together with black, it is one of the best colors for accessories, like handbags, gloves, and shoes, because it is a natural color.

Buttons

Recently buttons have become very important in fashion, but they have always been the most convenient way to open and close a garment. They can be a very important ornament and they can help to give the right importance to a dress.

Sometimes one button well placed gives a better effect than an eruption of buttons.

Camouflage

Since the days of Adam and Eve women have been using a thousand and one tricks of dressing to make the best of themselves.

Camouflage is very, very important. Most of the art of couture is the art of camouflage because perfection is rare in this world and it is the couturier's job to make you perfect.

In the hands of an expert such a lot can be done with clever cutting and a little padding. Coats and suits, especially, can be "built" on a person.

Checks

I love checks. They can be fancy and simple; elegant and easy; young and always right.

Right from the earliest days of weaving, checks have been popular and they are always in fashion.

And there are so many styles of checks to choose that there will be one to suit every age and figure.

The young and gay will have check gingham frocks … the petite woman will choose tiny checks … the older woman will have a broken check in a soft silk or woolen material … for the country there are beautiful, classic check tweeds.

For summer evenings fine cotton in pastel colored checks is very dainty … and for holiday time checks are very gay for accessories—gloves, scarves, etc.

Chiffon

One of the loveliest of all materials. And one of the most difficult to use. In French "chiffon" means "rag," and I must say that a chiffon dress that is not well made easily looks like a rag! Chiffon needs to be used in a perfectly feminine fashion; and draped with what we call in France *doigts de fée*—fairy fingers. If you are not a very experienced dressmaker my advice to you would be to avoid using chiffon for frocks; of course, you can easily use it for a little scarf.

Blouses, too, are very charming in chiffon—especially for the older woman—and they are lovely in soft neutral shades of gray, beige, and oyster.

Chiffon is essentially a feminine material; if you have a frock or a suit that presents rather a hard look you can always use chiffon to soften the effect.

Coats

This is the garment that has kept the original function of clothes—to keep you warm.

In the Stone Age women loved to keep warm with furs—and today the best materials for coats are those nearest to furs; this means wool and velvet.

Silk coats are summer coats; one wears them for adornment rather than for practicality. Personally, I don't like seeing women in town without a coat.

. . . Dior's fitted coats are ideal for the petite woman. This one, in dark gray, has an unusual tie fastening.

C

Coats can be either fitted or loose, whichever is your personal choice. But above everything they must be practical. Practical in color and practical in style.

Cocktail Frocks and Hats

Cocktail dresses are especially elaborate and dressy afternoon frocks. But avoid the mistake of dressing for a cocktail party as you would for a dinner party. This is wrong.

I think the most convenient type of cocktail frock is a little strapless or very décolleté design with a little bolero on top. Then with the bolero you look well dressed for the street; and without the bolero you will be right for formal occasions.

...Cocktail frocks. A matching jacket-bolero tops a décolleté frock in Dior's favorite black.

. . . *Cocktail hats.*
Can be large or small,
fancy or simple, and
any color you like.
Black is Dior's choice
for this tiny oval hat
worn well forward.

For cocktail dresses you can choose fairly rich materials—taffetas, satins, chiffons, or wool (wool is excellent) and here again you will choose a dark color, preferably black if it suits you. But leave very rich embroideries or heavy brocades for evening gowns.

Cocktail hats are the fanciest hats of all. You can have them in any materials; they may be embroidered, covered in flowers, feathers, or ribbons. You can have a big hat or a small one (but choose a small one if you are going to be in a small space!)

You can have any color—you can let your imagination and femininity take over!

Collars

The work of a collar is to frame your face. And big or small, high or low, its proportions must always be very well studied.

It is extraordinary how many different kinds of collars have been invented out of such a small piece of material.

The famous "little white collar" is, of course, very nice and youthful; but don't use it too much because it may sometimes look cheap. And never wear a white collar twice—it must be spotless.

A casually knotted scarf collar for a plain blouse.

A scarf collar trims a white satin blouse.

Detachable ribbed collar to wear on a plain jersey.

A neat tie collar for a plain white blouse.

Black piping edges the collar of a suit.

"Little boy" collar made of tiny white feathers.

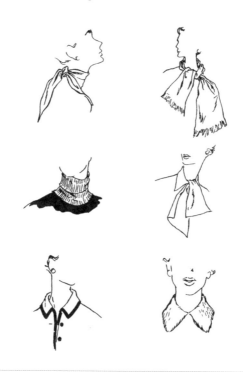

Pay great attention to the shape and the fit of your collar; an ill-fitting collar will throw the whole of your frock out of balance.

Usually little collars are young-looking and bigger collars, especially draped ones, are more dignified. If you want to look young you will choose a crisp material, too—like piqué. If you want to look sweet you will select a fine piece of lace (perhaps you will have made it yourself).

If you have a long neck you may have an upstanding "highwayman's" collar, or a mandarin collar. If you have a short neck you will choose a long, narrow collar.

Colors

Colors are wonderful and glamorizing—but they must be used with care.

Even the prettiest color, if you wear it every day, will lose its effect. Color needs change. We wouldn't appreciate blue skies if they were always blue, it is the clouds, the ever-changing scene, that makes the sky so beautiful.

Nothing about Nature is ever static ... the countryside changes daily; the sky changes hourly; and the sea is never the same for a minute.

Color may be used in touches if you wish to change the look of your clothes. An emerald scarf ... one brilliant red rose ... a sunshine yellow stole ... royal blue gloves.

But if you have only a small wardrobe restrict your colors to your accessories.

A colored frock can look very gay and attractive, but you can easily get tired of it, and you will not get as much wear out of it as you would out of a little black or navy blue frock.

You understand that when I talk of colors I mean the bright colors; not the neutral colors like gray, beige, black, or navy which may be worn every day. But even those shades must be selected to match your skin, your hair, and your eyes.

For instance, few shades of beige will suit someone with gray hair because beige and gray are too similar in quality. Those of you with gray hair should choose either gray or navy blue or, of course, black.

For summer cotton frocks, of course, you will be able to choose the gayest colors in the world—because you will have many of them.

But when you are choosing good quality clothes that you will wear a great deal, stick to the neutral colors. You must take great care, too, in choosing your colors for accessories.

Two colors in any outfit are quite enough. And two touches of any one color are enough.

A hat, gloves, scarf, and belt all of the same bright color is ruin; it merely gives a spotted effect. Whereas a colorful hat and scarf lead the eye to a focal point in an outfit.

Good planning is very necessary to good dressing.

Corduroy

Corduroy has been, and is still, always in fashion because of the great quantity of shades and the great convenience of it—it is extremely practical.

I like it very much because it is just as useful as woolen materials and it gives a different element to your wardrobe. You can use corduroy for both suits and frocks—and coats too, if you wish. It is always very young-looking.

Both in velvet and corduroy you get the most wonderful colors—soft colors and brilliant colors. But it is rather a rich material so should be used for very simple styles.

You can also use corduroy where you would use velvet to trim a suit or a coat—its good texture contrasts well with a smooth woolen material.

Cosmetics

Cosmetics play a very big part in the secret of beauty, but they mustn't show. Too much make-up is now very old-fashioned. You don't have to be under strong lights like an actress on a stage, so there is no need to be made up like one.

The most natural make-up is best, and except for lipstick it must not show. Brightly colored nail varnish is all right if you like it, but personally I prefer natural colors.

Crepe

For a time crepe has been out of fashion but now it is back again because it is very convenient and has sometimes the look of wool, but not the warmth.

For frocks you can use soft crepe in almost all the ways you would use wool—you can drape it or pleat it or gather it; it is very versatile.

For springtime I love a pleated dress in a crepe of pastel shade.

Cuffs

Cuffs do for your hands what a collar does for your face—they make a frame and a background for lovely wrists and fingers.

And I would say the same about white cuffs that I do about white collars. They are very nice but they can look cheap.

Cuffs can give great importance to a sleeve, whatever the length. But be careful when you add cuffs to long sleeves. They should not be so long that they cover the wrist as this looks ageing.

I love cuffs on suits and coats as well as on frocks. But I do not think they should be too fancy—just a little turn-back cuff is best for my taste.

They can be in the same material or a contrasting one; and they can be the same color or a contrast. But, as I said before, beware of introducing too many patches of color. If you have a contrasting collar and cuffs on a frock, that will be enough color for the whole outfit.

Detachable ribbed cuff.

Small folded blouse cuff.

Narrow cuff of white feathers. Deeply pointed turn-back cuff on a long-sleeved blouse.

Neat little buttoned blouse cuff.

A full-sleeved coat has a gathered-in cuff line.

Darts

Are extremely important to the cut of a dress, but it is bad to use too many. It is not by putting in a dart that you will correct a bad fitting.

A good fit must be obtained in the first place by the way you use the grain of your material.

Darts are only necessary to fit your bodice. Generally two or four darts are enough to give you an excellent fit. Avoid making them too big; it looks ugly.

Nicely cut clothes must be cut with the fewest possible seams.

Never choose a frock or pattern with many darts and seams. They are difficult to make; and they will not necessarily wear well. When you are making a frock, pay special attention to choosing a design with few darts and few pattern pieces for the main part of the frock.

. . . Darts are cleverly used in this short evening frock to create back fullness without gathers.

Day Frocks

There are some women who look best in suits, but there are others who cannot wear suits, especially if they are very small or have short legs.

For them, I advise the wool frock—the day frock. You can wear it every day, every month of your life, so choose a simple, classic style in a neutral color and ring the changes with carefully chosen accessories.

. . . Day Frock.
A Dior day frock in
a neutral "tobacco"
shade. Very simple
in line, it has a high,
round neckline and
loose comfortable sleeves.

D

Always buy frocks of the best quality wool you can afford. Cheap woolen material is not really cheap because it quickly becomes shabby and will be worn out before you have had it more than a few months.

A classic wool frock in black, or navy or dark gray should last you several years.

If you are young, choose a style with a full skirt, neat bodice, and high-fastening neck. If you are not-so-slim I would advise a cross-over bodice and a straight skirt with one or two pleats to give movement.

A V-neck is always flattering—and essential for those of you who are big in the bust; while a little drapery is good if you are a little too thin. But be careful and do not choose anything at all fussy because then you will be tired of your frock before it is worn out.

Décolleté

Since the days of Eve, décolleté frocks have always been attractive. Small or big, décolletés are always feminine.

If you are tall, choose a wide décolleté. If you are a bit plump, a deep décolleté is good for you.

Whatever neckline your frock has, make sure it is not so high that it covers your collar bone. The only exception is when you wear sweaters—they can be as high as you wish.

Personally, I take great care in designing new and feminine décolletés. Nothing is more becoming. Nothing is more feminine. Nothing is more attractive.

. . . Décolleté. A simple and graceful neckline to a black silk afternoon frock.

Detail

I hate detail. I love accents or little touches but they must always be important—not insignificant. The small detail is something very cheap and not elegant at all.

Although it has another meaning—you must be elegant in every detail of your dress from head to foot. Then detail is important.

Dots

I would say the same about dots as about checks. They are lovely, elegant, easy, and always in fashion. I never get tired of dots.

Tiny dots are most suitable for petite figures. Big coin dots are good for tall people. And if you are not-so-slim you need to choose lighter dots on a dark background and not vice versa.

Dots are lovely for holiday clothes—cotton frocks and beach outfits—and they are gay, too, for accessories. According to their color, so they can be versatile ... Black and white for elegance; soft pinks and blues for prettiness; emerald, scarlet, and yellow for gaiety; beige and gray for dignity.

Dressing gowns

I think a dressing gown or housecoat is a very important garment in your wardrobe and too many women neglect it.

Our mothers used to take great care about dressing-gowns and they were quite right; because it is a gown in which your family see you every morning ... it is the first thing you wear to start the day, and it is so important to look always right especially in the intimacy of your home.

If you live a life of luxury (or for a special holiday), you may have one of those wonderful chiffon dressing-gowns which make you look so beautiful. But if you live a strict life, tweed or surah or wool, and cotton in summer, are by far the best.

I think with a dressing gown, too, a woman can indulge in a little femininity. Although it must above all be practical, don't let it be too severe. A little frilling or velvet trimming is good on a woolen dressing gown.

Earrings

Except in the country I always like to see women wearing earrings. They give a nice finishing touch. They need not be very elaborate; in fact little gold ones, or pearls or single jewels make charming earrings. For evenings, of course, they can be much more ornate.

I always ask my models to have pierced ears.

Elegance

This is a word that would need a book to give it its right definition! I will only say now that elegance must be the right combination of distinction, naturalness, care, and simplicity. Outside this, believe me, there is no elegance. Only pretension.

Elegance is not dependent on money. Of the four things I have mentioned above, the most important of all is care. Care in choosing your clothes. Care in wearing them. Care in keeping them.

Embroidery

One of the most beautiful things done by the hand of woman. But one of the most dangerous to use with elegance. I don't like embroidery on day clothes—unless it is very, very simple.

If used discreetly it is good for cocktail dresses and in a more elaborate fashion it is wonderful for evening clothes. For a dinner party a short embroidered dress may be very nice, but you must only wear embroidery on suitable occasions, otherwise it is pretentious.

You can use embroidery:

On a blouse—on the collar or to decorate the front, but it must be done with the finest silks and, unless you have a very sure color sense, it is wiser to embroider only with one color.

On a skirt sometimes for a gay holiday skirt it is possible to choose a dark gray or black, full cotton skirt and add some bold embroidery design in brilliant colors. But this sort of thing is only for the young ones!

. . . Embroidery can be used lavishly on evening clothes. Dior's short evening frock of rich, red satin is embroidered all over with sapphire-blue brilliants.

E

On an evening dress—embroidery looks wonderful ... embroidery with silks and jewels and sequins. They give a rich, luxurious look that is so attractive in an evening gown.

On a cocktail dress—sometimes it is nice to have a little embroidery on the collar or pockets of a frock—but, remember, only a little.

Emphasis

If you have a particularly outstanding feature it is always a good thing to emphasize it. In fact the whole of fashion is emphasis—emphasis on woman's loveliness.

. . . Emphasis. A lovely collar emphasizes a lovely face. Dior gives a black velvet evening jacket a collar of black satin. The little hat is exquisitely embroidered in coral.

If you have lovely hands the cuffs on your sleeve will emphasize them as long as they are the right length—they should come just above the wrist bone.

All collars emphasise a pretty face because they make a frame for it.

Almost every frock is cut to emphasize a tiny waist—and a belt, either narrow or wide, helps to do this also.

Good ankles are emphasized most by those "ballet" length skirts and the fuller they are the greater the emphasis.

. . . Emphasis on lovely legs calls for pretty shoes. These are from the range designed by Christian Dior and Roger Vivier.

Ensembles

A very elegant way of dressing is to have a coat and dress matching together, making an ensemble—and I believe the British women, especially, like them.

For an ensemble the frock should be fairly simple and

. . . Ensemble. Dior teams a dark gray frock with a coat of thick, caramel-colored wool. Caramel hat and creamy-beige gloves complete the color scheme. See page 36.

the coat can be either fitted or loose, according to your taste. It can also be either long or short.

An ensemble really takes the place of a suit but it is not so practical, because you cannot so easily change its appearance. With a suit you can sometimes wear a tailored blouse and sometimes a fussy one and combined with different hats, the effect will be quite different.

An ensemble can be worn only one way. Nevertheless, there are people who do not look their best in suits and if you are one of those I recommend an ensemble.

As to colors, I would say the same things I say about suits—choose a dark, convenient color like black, gray, navy blue—or beige. Because you will have to wear your ensemble often and these are the colors you will not tire of easily. Also they are good background colors for gay accessories.

Ermine

The emblem of purity and of royalty. In normal use, ermine gives a lovely touch of white in winter, when it is used as a collar or hat. Of course, for evening, an ermine bolero or coat is wonderful.

Faille

A lovely silk material less shiny than satin and a little more easy to wear and more slimming. It is the same kind of material as ottoman, grosgrain, and poult.

Faille is difficult to work because it crinkles easily, so it should be avoided by inexperienced dressmakers.

Feathers

Feathers are lovely on a bird and glamorous on a hat, but they must be used with great discrimination. They can look lovely but they can also look ridiculous.

Worn by an Indian chieftain in the right setting they look most dignified. With care, a woman may wear them in an elegant and distinguished way, too. Always choose small feathers—and dainty ones; big ones look clumsy and unfeminine.

. . . Feathers form the crown of this glamorous fur hat. They are tiny yellow ones to match the yellow velvet coat with which the hat is worn.

Fichu

A little triangle, or square piece of material folded into a triangle—very elegant for evening dresses and, in the fashion of today, fichus have a tendency to take the place of stoles which can be rather cumbersome.

In fact, if you find it difficult to manage a stole and wear it elegantly, I would advise you to choose a fichu instead. They may be fringed or embroidered and they can be of many materials.

Wool for warmth and to wear with woolen day frocks. Silk, satin, or even organdy for evening wear. They can be in dark colors or tweed colors for daytime; or you may have cheerful scarlet, green, or blue. In the evening, especially if you are young, you may choose a subtle, pastel color.

Fit

A good dress is, first of all, a well-fitted dress. I hate women who look as if they are dressed in a sack.

It is the fitting that helps to emphasize the loveliness of yourself and to hide the little faults you may have.

A good fit is something very difficult to obtain and you can never spend too much time on it. Usually a dress needs three fittings—sometimes it is necessary to give twice that number.

Be very careful with the grain of the material—this has to be studied very carefully. If the material is used the right way only the minimum number of darts and tucks are needed to get a good fit; if it is used the wrong way, then no amount of darting will give the fit you want.

So when you are making a frock, study your material and study the style you wish to make before you begin.

Flowers

After woman, flowers are the most lovely thing God has given the world. But being so sweet and so charming they must be used with care.

A flowered hat may be lovely or ridiculous. A flower in your buttonhole or in your belt or in your décolleté may be extremely nice

. . . Flowers can bring a touch of color to a dark dress. This spray from the Dior Boutique consists of pansies and mimosa.

—but choose a variety of flower and color to suit your personality.

Flowered prints I think are wonderful—silk prints in beautiful colors are lovely for afternoon suits, dinner frocks, or cocktail dresses.

In brilliant colors, too, flowered prints can be gay for holiday clothes.

. . . Flowers must be chosen to suit your personality. These two huge chrysanthemums from the Dior Boutique make a sophisticated evening head-dress.

. . . Feathers and fringe are used on these two Boutique skirts. The one on the left is entirely covered in tiny feathers of deep red. The one on the right is of green felt with a deep fringe trimming at the hem.

Fox

One of the most wonderful furs. Its only fault is to have been very much in fashion for so long that it has become rather commonplace.

Personally, I don't like coats made of fox; I think it is better fur for trimming. I like it used on coats, suits, and even with tweeds.

Frills and Flounces

A very romantic, simple and young way of retaining the fullness of a skirt. In recent years we have made great use of flounces, but now that fashion is turning toward slim skirts and slim hips, maybe flounces will be less used.

But, anyhow, I love them. And for a young girl's dress there is nothing nicer.

Fringe

Made in self-material or added as a braid, fringes are a very nice trimming. They give a natural finish to a stole or a scarf. And they can sometimes be used on a collar or on a pocket.

In the twenties they were used a lot to make entire dresses; that is why you have to be careful how you use fringes today—it is so easy to look old-fashioned.

Gloves

In town you cannot be dressed without gloves any more than you can be dressed without a hat. And for the evening nothing is more glamorous than very long gloves. You can choose them almost up to your shoulders if you wish, or, if you prefer to be more conventional, have them to just above your elbow.

You can use your gloves—both in the evening and in the daytime—to give that "little touch of color," but I don't like gloves to be too fancy. And, personally, I prefer the natural colors—black, white, beige, and brown.

Long gloves give great elegance to your hands and help to make them look slim and long. I like them simple—without too much decoration—but they need to be very well cut. And when they are made of leather the quality of the skins must be perfect.

I would prefer gloves made of fabric to leather gloves that are made of cheap skins.

. . . Gloves. Long suede gloves for evening. Gray satin shorties for evening. White kid for daytime.

"For evening," says Dior, "nothing is more glamorous than very long gloves."

G

Green

It is supposed to be an unlucky color. I think that is entirely wrong. I am superstitious and green has always been very good for me. And it is a lovely color and very elegant.

It is a color of Nature—and when you follow Nature for your color schemes you can never go far wrong. I love to see green used in every shade and in every material—from tweed in the morning to satin in the evening. There is green for everyone and for every complexion.

. . . Good grooming is easier if you keep to simple, uncluttered lines. Note the simple bodice on this Dior day frock.

Gray

The most convenient, useful, and elegant neutral color. Lovely in flannel, lovely in tweed, lovely in wool. And, if it suits your complexion, there is nothing more elegant than a wonderful, gray satin evening dress. For day frocks, suits, and coats it is ideal. I would always advise it. And many people who cannot wear black can wear a dark gray. (Remember that if you are big you must choose a dark gray and if you are petite a light gray is better for you.)

It is the most convenient color, too, for people who live half in town and half in the country because, with different accessories, a gray suit or coat may be equally suitable for both. It is a good color for accessories, too—almost anything goes with gray. White is perhaps the freshest and sweetest contrast but it is safe to say that whatever your favorite color is, you can safely wear it with gray.

. . . Gray is Dior's color choice for this charming wool afternoon frock. Note the simple neckline with its single button fastening.

Grooming

Grooming is the secret of real elegance. The best clothes, the most wonderful jewels, the most glamorous beauty, don't count without good grooming.

A pretty hat, crisp veiling and a simple hairstyle—all these add up to Grooming.

Hairstyles

Like everything that comes close to your face, your hairstyle is extremely important. And more important even than a hat or a collar because it is actually part of you.

You can never take enough care of your hair, but by that I don't mean that I like a very elaborate hair dressing. I hate it.

But good hair grooming—that is very necessary.

If you cannot go very often to the hairdresser choose a simple hairstyle that you can easily do yourself at home. And take care of it not only every day but many times a day.

I hate dyed hair. The color God has given to you is always the best and matches with your personality. It is never any good trying to be someone other than yourself.

You can improve yourself—by all means—but you will still be yourself and not somebody else!

If you get gray young, you will look very elegant and much younger with your hair gray than if you dye it. And after a certain age dyed hair does not deceive anybody.

. . . Hairstyles. The above sketches show the widely differing hairstyles chosen for three of Dior's mannequins.

Handbags

A very important accessory and used with not enough care by too many women.

You can wear the same suit from morning to dinner—but to be really perfectly dressed you cannot keep the same bag. For the morning it must be very simple and for the evening it must be smaller and, if you wish, a little more fancy.

Always the simplest and most classic handbags are the

best and the quality of the leather is very important. Inexpensive leather is not always inexpensive—it may prove to be very expensive because it may not last well.

If you can only have one or two handbags choose either black or brown because they will go with everything.

(In the daytime you can choose a bag with saddle-stitching but after luncheon or for a dressy luncheon I don't like them—I prefer unstitched bags in nice leather: calf, suede, crocodile, with a preference for suede.)

Evening bags may be embroidered or made in fancy materials—the same material as your frock, if you like. But if you want one evening bag to go with all your frocks have it in gold or gold material.

Don't forget, a bag is not a wastepaper basket! You can't fill it with a lot of unnecessary things and expect it to look nice and last a long time. Like all your clothes, a handbag needs *care*.

Have a place in it for everything—for your powder, notecase, purse, papers, etc. And don't mix your lipstick with your bank notes and your handkerchief.

... Handbags. These are two from the Dior Boutique. The one on the left is a daytime style in black suede, the one on the right is an evening bag in gold kid and faille with soutache embroidery.

Hats

Now we come to the most pressing problem of this time. Shall you or shall you not wear a hat?

I think that in town you cannot be really dressed without a hat. It is really the completion of your outfit and in another way, it is very often the best way to show your personality. It is easier to express yourself sometimes with your hat than it is with your clothes.

A hat can make you gay, serious, dignified, happy—or sometimes ugly, if you don't choose it well! A hat is the quintessence of femininity with all the frivolity this word contains!

To trim this hat of soft gray felt Dior uses a single bronze clip— part of a jewelry trio from his Boutique consisting of necklace, earrings, and clip.

Women would be very silly not to take advantage of such an efficient weapon of coquetry.

And with hats it is the same as with handbags and your clothes—always select the best possible materials.

In the winter velvet and good quality felts are lovely and very versatile and you can get wonderful, rich colors in those materials.

Fur is lovely, too—and besides being warm a little fur hat is very feminine. If you cannot afford a fur coat but yearn for some little fur for cold days, then, by all means, have a fur hat!

The line of a hat is just as important, too, as the line of your frock. Too many hats are just "shapes" cluttered up with numerous decorations in the form of feathers or flowers. If a hat has a good line it will still be attractive without any trimmings at all.

Equally, when you have a hat with a good line do not ruin it with a bunch of flowers that you have a sudden whim to wear!

For summer, little silk or straw hats are very nice—and I purposely say "little" because they are much more convenient to have than big ones. You quickly tire of hats with enormous brims and except on very still summer days they are difficult to wear elegantly—you do not always want to be holding on to the brim!

Of course on the right day and for the right occasion—like a garden party—nothing is nicer or more provocative than a really big hat.

For sport or in the country, I do not very much like hats—unless rain, wind, or a strong sun draws them back to their original use which is to cover the head.

Heels

Heels are the most important part of your shoes because your whole walk depends on your heels. Sometimes women who are not especially gifted physically get a reputation for elegance by the grace of their walk and movements.

Too high heels are vulgar and hideous—and uncomfortable, I should imagine. But too low heels can sometime give you a masculine look that is good only for sport and the country. Just as it is so often with everything, the medium course is best—and usually medium heels are best. But shoes are a very individual matter and you have to choose for yourself. Sometimes, for evening occasions, it is amusing to have shoes with colored heels but usually I prefer plain heels, the color of the shoes.

... Heels. Diamante decorates the very new heel-line of this gold kid evening shoe from the Christian Dior-Delman Boutique.

Hemlines

There's such a lot of talk about hemlines, but, personally, I think it is ridiculous to count in inches how far above the ground a skirt should be.

It is an individual matter. It depends on each woman and on her legs.

But to find *your* own skirt length depends very much on the style you wear and how tall you are.

And the only rule is that of good taste.

Hipline

Since the war, the hipline has been the focal point of fashion—in contrast to a small waistline. Recently the interest has risen up to the top of the bust and the hipline is kept natural except for bouffant skirts.

If you have a slim hipline you can wear any type of skirt—pencil slim, gathered, bouffant, or flared. But if you are not as slim as you would wish then you must avoid too much bunchiness in your skirts; never choose flounces or frills. And in your frocks choose a design with some width in the shoulders to give you balance.

. . . Hipline. If your waist and hip are slim—emphasize them! Dior shows you how to do it with a huge eye-catching bow on a black wool frock.

Holidays

Holidays are the time to wear very convenient, casual, and simple clothes; but it is never the time to wear fancy clothes which look like a masquerade.

You can wear skirts, or slacks, tweeds or cottons, sweaters or blouses; all the comfy, gay, and casual clothes you wish.

But you must always be elegant. And I would like to say now that I think British women know perfectly how to dress for sport and holidays. For these occasions all the world has to learn from them.

. . . Holiday Clothes. The attractive jacket on the left has back and sleeves in knitting but its front in wind-cheating suede.

Beige tweed is Dior's choice for the casual skirt which, like the jacket, is from his Boutique.

Individuality

Until the time we are converted into robots—and I hope this time will never come—individuality will be always one of the conditions of real elegance.

Even if you cannot always have your clothes made to measure, try to find the ready-mades that exactly fit your personality.

In this period of mass production you may always find in the great variety of what is offered to you, something that is really your type. Try to understand well what is your personality and never forget that individuality does not mean eccentricity.

No elegant woman follows fashion slavishly. If a particular new line does not suit you, then ignore it. There is no one line each new season, there are many lines—and it is up to you to exercise your own good taste in choosing the ones that are best for you.

A black and white checked lining and matching checked hat give a striking touch of individuality to Dior's black coat and frock shown on the previous page.

Interest

There has never been such interest taken in fashion as there is today. And fashion has never been so readily available to women throughout the world.

Not many years ago only a favored few were able to come to Paris and be dressed by the leading couturiers of the day—Vionnet, Worth, Chanel, etc. Today, through the fashion magazines, and the wholesale fashion houses, the creative art of the world's couturiers is readily available to every woman.

The Paris Collections are reported in such detail in the world's press that women many thousands of miles away from France know, within a few hours, all about the newest styles. They can copy the ideas of the men whose whole lives are devoted to fashion; they can pick and choose amongst many hundreds of different designs. They have a very great advantage over their grandmothers! But with all this wealth of fashion news and detail showered upon them the problem of the modern woman today is to use her own good taste and discretion to choose only those things that are good for her.

However much you admire a certain frock or coat on somebody else before you wear a similar one yourself you must think to yourself "What will this do for *me*?"

And unless it fits in with your personality, your age, your figure, you must choose something else.

Jackets

. . . Jackets. Dior chooses vivid red for a box jacket to team with matching frock and hat shown on the facing page.

The box jacket is almost as important as a suit and many women who are a little bit plump can use the box jacket instead of a suit. It hides everything and is always elegant and nice. I love box jackets.

They must always be worn with a slim skirt. With a pleated skirt it may sometimes be nice but it is very difficult to wear and I would not advise it.

A box jacket is often very convenient, too, because you can wear it over a slim skirt worn with a jumper and you can wear it for extra warmth with a woolen frock—or even a suit. Because a jacket is usually an "extra" in your wardrobe you can afford to choose a gay color—perhaps red or strawberry, royal blue, or emerald, according to your own personal taste.

Jewelry

Real jewelry is the highest point of great luxury. I always prefer the finest to the biggest. To wear a big diamond on your finger means only that you have a lot of money—it means nothing in elegance.

I think the quality of the stones, the design of the jewel, and the perfection of the workmanship, are much more important than the size of the stone.

In the last centuries there have been some wonderful jewels made only with gold and enamels. These are more beautiful than the biggest stones in the world because they are art and created.

But for those of you who do not have many real jewels a lot of use can be made of costume jewelry. It is a very nice way to give a sparkle to your clothes that is so becoming.

Costume jewelry is something quite different from real jewelry; the two must never be confused and never mixed together.

As a rule I would say use jewelry generously to get the most out of it. A many-stoned necklace of rhinestones for instance will look lovely with a décolleté frock for evening. It will go equally with a fine black knitted sweater for afternoons.

A lovely trio of necklace, brooch, and earrings in amber-colored stones.

Heavy gilt jewelry has been popular in recent years, too. It gives a nice, bright richness to your clothes. Generally speaking, the use of jewels is a question of taste and circumstance and social conditions and you must use your discretion.

At certain times for instance many rows of pearls look charming but they are ridiculous if you are going to do the shopping.

Like everything in fashion the question of taste is more important than money. Some people will always wear a brooch in the same place—at the neck of a frock or the lapel of a suit. Another woman with fashion sense will take the same brooch and pin it, with a colored chiffon scarf, to the hip pocket of her suit—it will look marvelous and be twice as effective.

. . . Jewelry. A heavy evening necklace in jet and brilliants—lovely to wear with black.

For daytime, Dior shows this neat little choker of dark green stones.

Suitable for day or evening—a two-strand necklace of mottled beads.

Key to Good Dressing

There is no key.

If there were it would be too easy, rich women could buy the key and all their fashion worries would be over!

But simplicity, grooming, and good taste—the three fundamentals of fashion—cannot be bought.

But they can be learnt, by rich and poor alike.

. . . The Key to Good Dressing is beautifully illustrated in the Dior outfit shown on the facing page— simple black suit, matching gloves and muff, and hat and scarf, in vivid cerise.

Neat black accessories with a suit of black and white tweed— essentially good taste.

Knitwear

In the twenties knitwear first came into haute couture fashion. It is still very elegant and it will last forever, I hope.

It is always very satisfying to make something with one's hands and that is, I think, why knitting is so popular. There is a great art in knitting beautifully. And a beautiful frock, knitted in fine wools in a delicate pattern is as great a work of art as a painting—and more practical!

To turn some balls of wool into a lovely frock is a great achievement!

. . . The Key to Good Dressing. A court shoe from the Christian Dior-Delman Boutique—the keynote is simplicity.

For both town and country wear I like jerseys. I like them in all colors. But a black jersey—in the softest wool (you see, as always, the finest quality is essential) is probably the most useful garment a woman can have in her wardrobe.

You never want to have jerseys in a too fancy design— a fancy stitch is enough in itself. Personally I do not think you can improve on the plain classic styles that go on for years and years.

And remember, with a long-sleeved jersey, as with all long sleeves, do not have them so long that they cover the wrist bone; it is unflattering. During recent years the standard of knitwear has improved enormously. You can get knitted things now that are right for every hour of the day. Dainty, elegant frocks for the cocktail hour and heavy, thick sports wear.

Lace

Originally beautiful and expensive handwork; now machinery has made it possible for every woman to have it.

I love lace for evening dresses ... for a cocktail frock ... or for a blouse. I am not so keen on it for trimmings—it easily looks old-fashioned. A little lace collar can look charming on a black frock but it must be chosen with discretion—you don't want to look like Little Lord Fauntleroy!

... Line. This Dior frock in black wool has a very simple line—neat, high neck, edged with white, tiny sleeves and a full skirt.

Under a black suit or with a full skirt for parties, a lace blouse can look charming. But being a rich and elaborate material it should only be used for very simple styles. When a fabric is fancy in itself it needs simplicity of design to show it to its best advantage.

It is the same with an evening dress—choose a style of great simplicity; no complicated drapes or complicated cutting.

Leopard

For a long time leopard has been used as a "sport" fur. Personally, I find it just as good for very dressy coats and as nice for the evening as for the daytime.

But to wear leopard you must have a kind of femininity which is a little bit sophisticated. If you are fair and sweet don't wear it.

Linen

In spite of the great competition of cotton, I think linen is the top material for summer. It is cool and fresh and at the same time just as rich as silk or wool.

L   71

Linen gives to the color a subtleness that no other material has. And as well as looking nice, linen is a very convenient material—hard-wearing and easy to handle.

It tailors well—like wool—and is equally suitable for suits, frocks, or even summer coats.

In hot weather for town wear nothing is nicer than a linen suit in a dark color—preferably black. In the country there are hundreds of lovely shades of light and bright colors to choose from.

. . . Leopard-printed silk is the fabric used for this gay sports shirt from the Boutique.

L

Lingerie

I would say the same about lingerie as about lining—use materials of first-class quality. Lingerie must always be very refined. This does not mean that it must be all embroidered or covered with lace; but it must be well cut and of the finest fabric.

Our mothers used to spend a lot of time and money on lingerie and I think they were right. Real elegance is everywhere, especially in things that don't show.

It is psychological, too. Even if you had on the most beautiful frock, you could never feel your best if you knew that your lingerie was not equally beautiful.

Also, your frocks cannot hang perfectly unless your lingerie is cut to fit you perfectly underneath. Lovely lingerie is the basis of good dressing.

Linings

These are very important in the modern way of making clothes. What is inside is sometimes more important than what appears!

A good suit is not made only by the material you see but more by the inter-lining, which gives it the shape. Most dresses are now made in this way.

The lining, properly speaking, is of great importance for coats and jackets. It is extremely elegant to have a lining which matches with the dress or blouse you wear.

Never use cheap materials for linings—it is false economy. As a general rule everything that does not show —or shows very little—should be made of just as good, if not better, materials than what is apparent.

Materials

You can never take too much care of the materials you choose to make a dress, and it is one of the greatest difficulties of the couturier to find the right material to express his idea.

Sometimes to make a little black dress we have to compare twenty or thirty different qualities of black wool. You should take equal care when choosing material for a frock yourself.

As well as making sure it is a good color—which means you must see it by daylight as well as by electric light—study the weight and texture of the material and see that it is suitable for the design you have in mind.

It is wrong to think that a design can be made up in any material. A wrong choice may ruin the best design. That is why, if you are making a frock from a couture pattern, unless you are very sure of your taste, choose a material as near in weight and design as the original. You can be sure that the couturier has spent much thought before he made his choice and you will be wise to take advantage of his experience.

As a general rule, remember that when you have chosen a complicated design you will need a simple fabric. When you have a rich and luxurious fabric, have a simple design.

Some materials are much more difficult to work with than others—finely woven woolens, cotton, linen, and pure silk are usually easy.

Chiffon is more difficult and, as I said before, should only be used in the hands of an experienced dressmaker. Velvet can sometimes be a little difficult, too.

Velvet, pale beige, and heavily jeweled, combined with absolute simplicity of line, spells perfection in the evening gown and matching stole shown on the facing page.

Of all fabrics jersey—both silk and woolen jersey—is the easiest to drape, while fine wool and heavy linens are best for tailoring.

Don't forget, too, when choosing materials that little patterns are best for little people, while tall people (not fat) can carry off the bolder patterns. It is the same with a material like gray flannel, you should choose the color according to your size—light gray for petite figures; dark gray for the not-so-slim.

Wool—thick, soft, and pale pink is Dior's choice for this beautiful coat.

Tweed is the perfect material for this gray suit, worn with black accessories.

M

Mink

The best and nicest of all the furs. A mink coat in certain countries is synonymous with a certain standard of life and of social standing. Of course mink is a wonderful fur, but choose it not for the price but for its quality. It is generally said that light mink is better than dark. But, as with all furs, I think that the best for you is the one which matches your complexion.

If you have dark hair, ordinarily a dark fur is best for you, and vice versa.

Net

. . . Net is Dior's choice for this lovely evening frock in stark white accented with black.

Net is the ideal material for a certain kind of romantic evening dress. It is especially good for young girls and lovely for a first evening dress.

But you must always use plenty of it. A net frock should have at least three layers of net and be very full. (Net is such an inexpensive fabric it is not extravagant to have many yards of it in one frock.)

Much of the charm of net is the impression of lightness and transparency it gives. A net frock must always look very fresh and crisp. Nothing looks so poor as a crinkled net frock. (And net is so easy to iron there is no reason why it should not always look perfect.)

When I say you must always have three layers of net I do not mean that they must necessarily be all the same color—sometimes it is nice to have say, three shades of blue; or white and two pale shades of gray. When you mix colors be very careful—sometimes pale pinks and blues can look a little too sweet.

When you have a net evening dress its charm lies in the big, full skirt and to balance it you need only a very simple bodice that can very often be made in a different material.

Neutral Shades

Neutral shades are good for a lot of country or informal suits and dresses. Personally I love gray, which suits almost everyone.

And gray, like black, is such a convenient color. Almost all colors look nice with it—gray and white, gray and yellow, gray and scarlet. If you have a gray suit or coat you can choose your favorite color to wear with it.

There are two ways to select the right shade of gray for yourself. You can go by the color of your eyes or your size.

If you have blue, hazel, or light gray eyes then a light shade of gray will suit you.

If you have dark gray eyes or brown eyes, then a dark gray will be best for you.

Petite people look nicest in a very light gray; bigger people need a dark shade.

Beige is a charming color, too, and can look extremely elegant. But it is more difficult to wear than gray. To wear beige you must have a very good complexion. If you are inclined to look a little sallow then you must keep beige well away from your face. Like gray, there are many different shades—and when selecting the color best for you apply the same principle, the smaller, the lighter; the bigger, the darker!

Nonsense

In fashion, nonsense is to wear a big straw hat with a raincoat. A raincoat with an evening dress. Brogues with a cocktail dress. High heels with slacks. Velvet after March. Lace with tweed. I could write a book about nonsense in fashion! Too many women forget that even the most extreme fashion must be sensible in a way. Good fashion is always natural evolution and based on common sense.

I dislike trick fashions—designed only for publicity's sake. They may be eye-catching but they are never elegant.

Nylon

Personally I have never made a dress in nylon. I think this material has to be studied for years before it will be very good for dresses, except for a kind of sport or beach clothes.

But I do know that nylon is very convenient for lingerie and from the point of view of laundering I appreciate its usefulness.

Occasions

... *Occasions. A wedding is a great Occasion. Whether you are the bride or bridesmaid you must look your loveliest. Here is a bridesmaid dressed by Christian Dior in a very simple and utterly charming white frock. Her bouquet is of white lilies of the valley, her little jeweled hat is worn straight on her head.*

Generally it is very bad to be overdressed, but I think that in certain circumstances it is very impolite and wrong to be underdressed.

If you have to play a leading part on an occasion, you must have special clothes.

Who would imagine a great wedding with the bride in a gray suit? And it is as important for the bridesmaids to be well dressed as it is for the bride; they must always be a little less grandly dressed than the bride and must complement her.

The Coronation was an instance when it was very necessary to dress on a grand scale—and how wonderful the robes and tiaras looked!

Today, when clothes are so versatile, there is no reason why you cannot be suitably dressed for most evening occasions even if you do have to go straight from the office.

Those little frocks with detachable boleros, with a change of hat, enable you to be correctly dressed throughout the day.

Older Women

I have said before that today there need be no old women. There are only women who are older than others.

After a certain age—or more often after a certain size—forget the little girl fashions; too long hair, too pretty styles. But this does not mean that you have always to wear black, gray, or brown.

I know many women who are really elegant when dressed for summer or for evening in pale colors like pink, pale blue, or white.

Just as you must avoid childish clothes, so you must avoid too-old colors, like purple, and too-old fabrics, like brocades and a certain kind of black and gray lace.

Nothing is prettier than gray hair. And by the time a woman's hair is gray she has usually acquired a charming kind of dignity and femininity. So she will choose elegant clothes with soft lines—nothing too sophisticated or too masculine.

Ornaments

We live in a period where ornaments, whether in fashion or in furnishing, are usually superfluous. Anything with no basic reason is unnecessary. We love purity in line and anything that breaks it is wrong.

Ornaments can do nothing for a frock if they aren't part of the whole design. And if the basic line of a garment is wrong no amount of ornament will cover it.

Beware of adding "bits and pieces" to a frock—it seldom works. If you don't like the frock as it stands in the first place, don't buy it.

Padding

A way of correcting and accentuating certain parts of the dress that fashion wishes to emphasise. For years shoulder pads were a necessity for suits but now that the fashion is to look more natural, there is less need for padding—you have only to use it if your shoulders are too sloping.

Padding can be useful, too, in correcting minor figure faults—but only in the hands of an experienced dressmaker.

Perfume

Since the beginning of civilization perfume has always been used and has been considered an essential part of woman's attraction.

. . . Perfume. The loveliest of all is "Miss Dior."

When I was young, women used much more perfume than they do now and I think that was wonderful and I regret that more women don't use it lavishly now.

Perfume, like your clothes, can so much express your personality; and you can change your perfume with your mood.

I think it is as important for a woman to have beautiful perfume as it is for her to have beautiful clothes. And do not think that you need to have perfume only on yourself; your whole house can smell of it, and especially your own room.

Persian lamb

Persian lamb is always fashionable. Ever since I was a young boy I have seen Persian lamb worn in different ways. It can look very nice and young—but it must be used simply. Avoid too-elaborate styles; Persian lamb is, in itself, a little fancy and so needs to be used in a simple way.

I love Persian lamb trimmings for suits and coats—very elegant.

Petticoats

With full dresses, the petticoat has gathered great importance. Nothing is duller than a dress that should have a petticoat worn underneath, worn without it. The material hangs poorly on the body.

Stiffened petticoats give a dress a very charming and feminine silhouette and should really be considered as part of the dress.

If you make yourself a new frock that needs a petticoat of a certain fullness, it is essential to make one especially—it is no good feeling that something you have already got will do, because it probably won't.

Pink

The sweetest of all the colors. Every woman should have something pink in her wardrobe. It is the color of happiness and of femininity.

I like it for blouses and scarves; I like it for a young girl's frock; it can be charming for suits and coats; and it is wonderful for evening frocks.

Piping

A way of trimming sometimes necessary if you have made a cut in the material (as you do for a buttonhole). I prefer piped buttonholes for women's clothes—and stitched ones are usually reserved for men's clothes. Another way of using piping is to emphasize a line—and this can be very effective. It is especially good for the Princess Line I mention on page ninety-one. Sometimes you can use the same material for piping and sometimes a contrast both in color and material.

Piqué

A lovely cotton material. For a long time we used it only for trimmings, now we love to use it for dresses and it has been so greatly improved in recent years that it is now suitable for suits and coats as well.

But it still remains a favorite fabric for trimmings—collars, cuffs, piping, etc.

Pleats

For years pleats have been, and will continue to be, a high point of fashion. I love them because they are feminine, energetic and moving. They always give a look of simplicity that I like very much. They are very young.

With pleats you may put the greatest fullness in a dress without making it look bunchy. They are very slimming and becoming to almost every woman.

They are very versatile, too—you can have box, accordion, unpressed, inverted, and sun-ray pleats—and they all have their uses.

Pockets

Firstly a very useful part of a dress; but now very often used like an ornament or a way to break up the silhouette.

Pockets are a very convenient way to emphasize a bust or hip line—and two vertical pockets are very good for giving a narrowing effect on the bust or hips.

And with a pocket you can easily give a nice touch of color to your outfit—by putting a handkerchief of light material in it.

There's another point, too—pockets are very useful to help you to do something with your hands if you are embarrassed and don't know what to do with them.

... Pockets. Dior uses a neat slit one for a tailored suit and a large patch pocket for a wool frock.

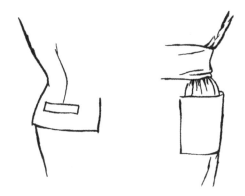

Princess Line

Because of its long lines the Princess Line is slimming if you are plump and it gives you height if you are small. So no wonder it is popular!

Purple

Purple—king of colors; but it has to be used with great care because it is not young looking. And it is not very gay.

But if you are young enough you may wear a purple coat in wool or a purple velvet dress and look wonderful in it. Again, purple is a color that needs a good complexion. And usually, I think, it looks best on people who are very dark or very fair. But it is full of dangers—and not very convenient because you may easily get tired of it.

Quality

Quality is essential to elegance. I will always put quality before quantity.

Whether you are buying or making clothes always choose the finest materials you can afford. It is always best to have one frock of good quality material rather than two of cheap fabric.

Good quality materials are not an extravagance—they will give you years of wear. Whether it is leather for gloves and shoes; felt for hats; or cloth for frocks, it always pays to have the very best quality you can afford.

Quilting

Quilting can sometimes make a nice winter lining for an overcoat; and if you wish you can choose a contrasting color—with a dark colored coat a bright red or blue that matches your frock is very cheerful.

Avoid using quilting as a trimming—it looks cheap. And in any form it is dangerous for a plump person.

Recently quilted skirts have been very popular and I think they are quite gay for teenagers—I would not advise them if you want to dress really elegantly.

Rainwear

Like everything functional, the simple and necessary lines of the raincoat are best. For years they always had to be made in rather drab materials, but now so many lovely fabrics are waterproofed that the raincoat may be made in almost every material.

Even so, a raincoat cannot be treated in the same way as an ordinary coat, because its main function is to protect you from the rain. Therefore it is essential that it closes well from neck to hem and does not have sleeves that are too wide.

Rayon

Rayon is now used as a material in its own right—and not just as a copy of other materials. And I think that in that way rayon is good; there are some materials which can only be made with rayon—like certain satins. But when rayon is used as a substitute, say, for pure silk, then naturally it is only second best.

Red

A very energetic and beneficial color. It is the color of life. I love red and I think it suits almost every complexion. It is good for any time, too .

Bright reds—scarlet, pillar-box red, crimson, cherry are very gay and youthful. And perhaps a red that is a little more somber is better for the not-so-young—and the not-so-slim, too!

But there is certainly a red for everyone; and if you do

not choose to have a whole frock or suit of red, then you may use it instead for accessories—a red hat to wear with an all-black or gray outfit is good; or a red cravat of heavy silk with a cream frock; or a red umbrella with a gray coat.

In winter I think a red coat is very nice because it is such a warm-looking color; and if most of your frocks and suits are in neutral shades a red coat will go very well with them.

. . . Red lends drama to this Dior evening gown and stole to match.

. . . Red gives piquancy to Dior's neatly tailored wool suit.

R

Ribbon

A little bow of ribbon has always been one of the favorite and most feminine trimmings. It is rare when you don't find a little bow somewhere on a woman's clothes.

You can have bows in all sizes and in almost all materials; it is, I think, the prettiest way of fastening the neck of a frock or the sash.

There is definitely an art in tying a bow—and you cannot attempt to do it properly with creased ribbon.

As well as for making bows, ribbon is very useful for trimmings; not just for trimming hats, either. You can use it on sleeves, cuffs, jumpers, cardigans, collars, and sashes.

Sable

The queen of all furs. The most beautiful, the most expensive. The most becoming. I love it.

Satin

The most glamorous and at the same time the most convenient of fabrics for evening dresses. You can get the most lovely colors in satin. The rayon satin has a different quality from the silk satin and they are both very good, depending on their use. The rayon satin is a little stiffer and the silk is better to drape.

Scarves

. . . Scarves can give the final touch to your frock.

In many cases a scarf gives a final touch to a dress. But you have to experiment and try many different ways of wearing a scarf before you find the way that suits you best. It is a very personal matter; and what suits one woman will not necessarily suit another.

A scarf is to a woman what a necktie is to a man, and the way you tie it is part of your personality.

Seal

A charming fur for sports coats. Especially convenient for young girls. Don't ever make the mistake of wearing it with silk dresses or dressy suits.

Seasons

More and more in the world of fashion, we divide the year into three seasons instead of four, autumn and winter being considered together. Spring and summer being slightly different for two reasons—first, holidays need different clothes, and in the spring the difference of temperature requires lighter materials than you would have for the winter.

The real times for buying or making new clothes are in the spring and autumn—with a special season for holiday clothes in the summer.

. . . Seasons.
For summertime—
a pretty check
holiday frock from
the Boutique.

Separates

I love separates. They are charming, young, useful, and gay. And they allow a woman with a small income to have variety and ring the changes in her wardrobe.

They are especially nice in summertime—in linen, cotton, silk, or fine wool. Many of my frocks I make in two pieces, too, because it is more convenient.

With separates you can have the top and the skirt of either the same or of contrasting colors and materials. But almost always they should have a full skirt and a small waist with a nice belt.

For evenings separates look a little bit casual and, I think, are only suitable for holiday resorts.

Shoes

You can never take too much care in selecting shoes. Too many women think that because they are low down, shoes do not matter, but it is by her feet that you can judge whether a woman is elegant or not.

Very plain calf Court shoes are good with a day frock or suit.

Calf court again for afternoon. All are from the Christian Dior-Delman Boutique.

There are many different kinds of nice shoes, but they must always be well adapted to the dress you are wearing. Court shoes are good with everything.

I hate fancy shoes of any description; and except for evening I don't care too much for colored shoes.

The two essentials for shoes are—first, that they should be made of good quality leather or suede; and secondly, that they should be in a simple, classic style. Black, brown, white, and navy are really the best (but white shoes are inclined to make your feet look big).

The shape of the heels is important—except for the country and for sports the heels should not be too flat; and they should never be too high, they look vulgar. In any case the important thing is that they should be comfortable. Uncomfortable shoes make you walk badly and then the most beautiful frock in the world will be badly displayed.

Suede court shoes are lovely with an afternoon frock or silk suit.

If your feet are long don't try to hide the fact but try to find a shoe that makes your foot look narrow. Narrow feet always look nice.

Skin court shoes look attractive with a suit or top coat.

Shoulderline

For many years the shoulderline has been natural. Personally, I never liked those very square shoulderlines that are not feminine and are a little bit aggressive.

Of course the shoulderline changes slightly every year with the fashion, but a little bit of padding is always good if your waistline is not very tiny. The width on your shoulders will make it look smaller.

A perfect fit on the shoulders is vital for any garment. I would say that if a suit or a coat does not fit you properly on the shoulders, do not buy it.

Silk

The queen of all the materials. The most lovely, the most feminine, the most enchanting with all the qualities Nature gives to things that we cannot make ourselves.

You can wear silk from the afternoon until midnight. And you can wear it again from midnight until the time you get up because nothing is nicer than silk for nightdresses, too!

You can make every kind of frock in silk—tailored, shirt-waist frocks, beautifully draped afternoon frocks, cocktail frocks, and ball gowns.

It's lovely for suits—either patterned or plain—classic tailored styles or dressy, afternoon suits.

It's lovely for coats—those flowing duster coats that have recently been in fashion; or tailored fitted coats made in heavy silk.

It's lovely for blouses, for lining, for lingerie—it's the loveliest material.

Skirts

There are few women who can wear every type of skirt. Only those who have a slim waistline and no hips. The rest of you have to choose which suits you best—a full skirt or a straight one—and when you have found the right type of skirt, keep to it.

The simpler your skirt, the better fit it must be. A slim skirt must never be so straight that you cannot move in it—that is ridiculous. Like everything in fashion your clothes must always give you the feeling that they are easy to wear.

Full skirts, too, need to be well cut so that there is no bunchiness round the waist; for this reason a flared or pleated skirt is usually more flattering than a gathered one. If width is needed on the hips (perhaps to give emphasis to the waist) it is better to have controlled width in the form of padding rather than a quantity of material.

Pleated skirts are especially good because they give all the movement of a full skirt and yet allow a straight line.

Stockings

This is the nylon kingdom. Of course they must be good quality, that is common sense. Try to find a shade that matches with your skin. And remember that dark shades are slimming.

Between day and evening there is a difference in the thickness of your nylons—they should be finer and lighter in the evening.

Stoles

. . . Stoles. Dior chooses a beautiful transparent gold stole to partner his gold embroided black velvet evening gown shown on page 98.

Stoles have two uses. First to cover your shoulders if you are wearing a décolleté gown. And secondly if you don't feel dressed enough for the street a stole may take the place of a short jacket and give to your dress a street look.

If you are clever enough to drape a stole elegantly it helps you to move gracefully, but nothing looks worse than a stole hanging loosely on a dress. So if you cannot wear a stole well, leave them alone.

Stoles may be either in the same material or contrasting in both color and texture to the dress or suit you wear. For evening, light materials like net or organza are very feminine. And of course a fur stole is very warm and elegant.

Stripes

. . Stripes are difficult to use because you have to keep the grain of the material the same way in every part of the dress. In this Boutique frock Dior solves the problem by using them only for skirt and bodice trimming—the bodice itself is plain black.

A nice and convenient design for fancy material but very difficult to use because when you use stripes you have to keep the grain of the material the same way in every part of the dress.

If you use them vertically it is very slimming but difficult to make because of the darts and all the curves of the body.

Stripes used horizontally can be very charming but not for plump people because they are very shortening.

I would say: never try to experiment with stripes and if you are making a frock never try to adapt striped material to a pattern not especially designed for it.

Of course it is common sense to say that the width of the stripe must be according to your size. Tiny stripes for tiny people and so on.

. . . Stripes are gay—especially the black and white zebra stripes Dior uses for this amusing hat and muff set.

Suits

Since the beginning of this century suits have become more and more important in a woman's wardrobe. Today it is, perhaps, the most important garment you can have.

Although a woman's suit is a fashion that has been adopted from men, I do not like a suit to be made like a man's suit—it is too masculine. Both the material and the cut must be different.

You can find a suit to wear for almost every circumstance of this life, from morning to evening—not *for* evenings, though; I don't like suits at nighttime.

For daytime in town a dark suit in a smooth material is best; and if black suits you then choose black; the "little black suit" cannot be beat for elegance and usefulness.

Second to black come gray and navy; and then a dark green.

If you lead a "double life"—half in town and half in the country and want to wear the same suit in both places, then gray is the most convenient for you.

If you want a country suit you cannot do better than choose a suit made of one of those lovely tweeds for which your country is famous. British women wear tweeds beautifully—but they are sometimes inclined to choose a too masculine style. Tweed does not want anything at all fancy in the way of design, but at the same time there is no need to have it made like a man's suit.

For the summer, I think linen suits are very nice; either in dark colors, again for town wear, or in white or pastel shades for the country and seaside.

Linen tailors beautifully, like wool, and looks most elegant in a simple, classic style. For afternoons nothing looks lovelier than a silk suit and colorful silk prints are very popular just now. For special occasions like Ascot or a Palace Garden Party or for your "going-away" outfit in the summer I would advise a silk suit.

Personally, I prefer suits to have a fitted jacket, but if you prefer a loose jacket by all means have it.

Taffeta

A charming material for cocktail or evening dresses. It must be used in quantity—very full skirts for dresses—otherwise it can easily look poor.

Sometimes it can be used for blouses, but it is a little stiff and its best use is for evening time.

Tartan

This is perhaps the only one of the fancy materials that is perennial. Tartan appears every season in some shape or form and is always young and gay.

But it is something you have to be careful with. The traditional use for tartan is of course for Scottish kilts—and when it is used in other ways it can be a little theatrical.

Plaids are a different matter—they can be of any color and design; but tartans are authentic in both color and design.

. . . Tartan is used effectively for this Boutique frock. Made in a simple shirtwaist style, the colors in the tartan are green, black, and white.

Traveling

With our new way of living and traveling and so much air travel, your wardrobe has to be vastly different from our grandmothers' days when they took trunks and trunks to contain their clothes.

If you travel extensively you need special clothes that do not take up too much room, that don't crease too much, and don't weigh too much.

As for the clothes you wear while you are traveling, the two essentials are that they should be comfortable and not crease. Nothing is more practical than a classic camel-hair coat with a wool day frock in winter and perhaps a linen suit in summer.

. . . Traveling clothes should be comfortable. The beautiful Dior coat, shown on page 108, is in a thick soft wool, patterned in a bold check design in two tones of gray.

Trimming

Trimmings are often very charming but they have never made a dress. A good cut is essential and too much trimming is always wrong.

Trimmings of every description must be designed in the first place as part of the dress—it is very often disastrous to add them later.

Tucks

Tucks have been used a great deal between the two wars. Now the art of couture is more in the molding and in the use of the grain of the materials. But tucks are still attractive on blouses or for light crepe or chiffon dresses, especially for shirtwaist styles.

Tweed

The most popular of all the British materials. They have been copied in every country but have never been made better than in Great Britain.

In the last few years tweeds have extended their use even for dressy suits. I think they are extremely elegant. To wear them in the country is a "must."

At one time you could only get tweeds in a rather heavy weight but now you can get them in all weights and qualities and colors.

. . . Tweed in a very dark gray is Dior's choice for this frock from his Boutique. A white organdy dickie highlights the unusual neckline.

Umbrellas

With the convenience of modern life umbrellas are now used more like an accessory than a necessity—but with the difficulties of parking a car in big cities they will become more and more useful!

To be really elegant an umbrella should not be too fancy. I like them best in bamboo, leather, or wood. And they must match with your other accessories—handbag, gloves, etc.

It is a good idea to have one umbrella and many covers for it—then you can have a color that goes with every outfit.

Underskirts

The ideal material for slim underskirts is *crêpe de chine* which is slimming and soft. For the bouffant dress, net is perhaps one of the best because if it shows a little as you walk it is always nice to look at.

Petticoats are very feminine and as much care should be taken with their color and material as with your frocks.

They must always be cut with great care because very often the look of the dress is conditioned by the underskirt.

Variety

Of course the dream of every woman would be to change her clothes every day to look different always—but it is financially impossible and I don't even think it would be nice.

When you see a woman looking lovely in a beautiful dress you are only too pleased to see her looking like that again.

When you have a favorite dress there is no reason why you should not wear it often. It is much better to have few clothes but good ones—as I have said so often before. And you can always give variety to your basic suit and frocks with accessories, scarves, flowers, or jewels.

Veils

Very flattering but not always young. You must be careful how you use them—they are for a woman rather than a girl.

Veils should always be fairly simple—I don't like very fancy net. A few dots are nice or just a plain veil; and not too thick.

Veils of the same color as your hair are often very nice, even with a black hat. Beware of brightly colored veils, they are seldom attractive.

. . . Velvet is glamorous and charming when used the couture way—as for this loose coat of bright lemon yellow . . . light colors in velvet are rare and lovely—but a luxury.

Velvet

No material is more flattering than velvet. It is most becoming to the complexion. A trimming of velvet or a velvet collar can entirely change the look of a suit or a dress. It is always good to have velvet near the skin.

I like velvet trimming in any season—not just in winter —and it often looks nice with linen, even with organdy.

Velvet dresses and velvet coats are attractive, too, but after the first of March it is not right to wear them; it is typically the winter silk material. Black velvet is extremely slimming. Colored velvets are more difficult to wear, but all the dark jewel colors are charming. Light-colored velvets are more rare and they are not very convenient because they mark so easily; they are lovely but a luxury.

Velvet can make very lovely rich evening dresses; but be careful with them, they are inclined to be a little ageing.

Personally, I love a black velvet afternoon dress with, perhaps, a touch of white on the collar—it is sweet and feminine and becoming to all ages.

Velveteen

I love cotton velvet, but mainly for loose coats and jackets—it is difficult to tailor. For fitted suits or fitted coats and dresses use it only if you are very slim because it is fattening.

Velveteen can make gorgeous evening capes—loose ones hanging from your shoulders in a lovely line.

. . . Velveteen is tops for jackets—this one from the Dior boutique, zips neatly up the front.

Waistcoats

If you don't wish to wear a blouse with your suit a waistcoat makes a nice change and is very convenient and nice. It can give your suit a little touch of color that a scarf may give but it keeps tidy and allows you to unbutton the jacket of your suit.

With a plain dark suit, waistcoats give you the opportunity to wear something gay—a check waistcoat or a plaid one looks very gay, and you can have them in silk or wool.

Waistline

The waistline is the key of dressmaking because it gives a frock or a suit all the proportion. A small waistline gives to the curves of the feminine body all its charm and has always been the dream of every woman.

Sometimes fashion has changed the place of the waistline, but I think the natural place is really the best.

But if your waistline is too long or too short, you have to try to correct it to give a good proportion between your bust and your legs. With a belt or with darts or a button which indicates its place, you have to cheat to find the right and becoming proportion. And of course you have to select your clothes with this in mind.

If you have a short waistline avoid high belts or too much bodice interest. And avoid a very wide décolleté—deep ones are much better for you.

If you are very long waisted then the reverse is right for you—wide décolletés, wide belts, and big collars. Almost always it is nice to emphasize the waistline with a belt—

and it is important that your belt should be made to fit you, nothing looks worse than a long piece of leather belt hanging down.

The Way You Walk

Not so many years ago girls were taught how to walk and I think it was quite right. A lot of women today should go back to school again and learn the art of walking well because it is extremely important.

Many women have been known not for their beauty but their charm—and their only charm was the way they walked. It is not easy to walk with dignity and lightness.

Some people have a natural gift for moving gracefully. But if it does not come naturally to you then you have to cultivate the art. It is ridiculous to wear beautiful clothes and then slouch along or sit in a slovenly manner so that they quickly become creased like rags.

. . . The Way You Walk can make or mar your clothes—cultivate gracefulness.

Weddings

If you are playing a part in the ceremony you have to make an effort and be dressed especially for it. This doesn't mean that you have to be covered with feathers and wear a train as long as the bride wears.

But of course it is a question of circumstances and you have to dress according to where the wedding is being held—in the country … in town … etc.

I think silk or fine wool are the best materials—avoid brocades that are too elaborate. And as always I would advise simple clothes but with something different to make it special and distinguished from the ordinary guests.

Bridesmaids usually have to wear long dresses—especially if the bridegroom is in a morning coat or tails. I would object to coats worn with a long dress—but if it is cold you can always have a stole or a short jacket in fur.

If you are a wedding guest then you will want to wear something very special, too. But nothing too striking that will in any way detract from the bride—brown, gray, some greens and medium blues are usually the best colors.

And if you are going to wear a spray of flowers don't wear too much jewelry as well—or you may look a little bit like a Christmas tree!

White

White is more beautiful than any color for evening. At a ball there are always one or two white dresses that are outstanding. White is pure and simple and matches with everything. For daytime it has to be used with great care because it must always be really white and immaculate. If you cannot keep it so it is better not to have it.

But nothing gives the impression of good grooming and being well dressed more quickly than spotless white ... white collars and cuffs, a white cravat ... white buttons ... or a white hat, or gloves.

Winter Sports

Winter sports play a more and more important part in winter fashions. About real sports clothes I have nothing special to say. Only that they have to be convenient and simple to be really elegant.

And I prefer them dark; all the gaiety, if you wish it, brought with scarves and perhaps gloves and caps. "After-ski" clothes should be gay, simple, and young. Then you can use fancy belts and fancy accessories—but still with discrimination. I hate anything that looks like fancy dress just as much for winter sports as for beach clothes.

Wool

Wool shares with silk the kingdom of textiles. It may be worn at any time for both simple or dressy clothes and the only exception is a ball dress. Rough or smooth, dark or light, plain or fancy, wool materials come in a wonderful variety. And like silk it has wonderful natural qualities.

Always before you cut woolen material it has to be shrunk to avoid disappointment afterward. Wool has the great advantage over all other materials in that it can be worked with a hot iron and molded. That is why it is ideal for suits or very fitted dresses.

The more you can mold a material the less darts are needed to make the garment fit—that is why we use wool so often in modern fashions. It is typically the material of today.

. . . Winter sports. An après-ski (after skiing) jacket of white imitation lamb.

W

Xclusive

In these days it is very difficult to have something really exclusive; with the modern methods of producing and reproducing it is almost impossible to have a material made only for you and a dress designed especially for you. It is a great luxury.

But your way to be exclusive is to be yourself. To find in your personality the things that are different and that will make you different from everyone else.

And always you must be natural. I never like sophistication.

Although the scarf you wear may be one of thousands it can still be exclusive in the way you wear it! And exclusiveness is not a question of money.

Of course, if you make your own clothes it is easier to have something exclusive—but that does not mean that it will have any more value.

Xtravagance

The contrary of elegance. Elegance may be audacious but it can never be extravagant because extravagance is bad taste.

It is always better to err on the side of simplicity rather than be extravagant in your dressing.

Yellow

The color of youth and of the sun, and of good weather. A beautiful color for frocks and also for accessories and right for any time of year. But if you are fair haired or have a pale complexion you must be afraid of this color. I do not mean that you must avoid it altogether, but you must choose only the light shades, leaving the bright golden yellow for brunettes.

Just like the other colors, there *is* a shade of yellow for everyone—but you have to take the trouble to find it.

Yoke

A way of giving to the bodice necessary fullness, and, at the same time keeping the shoulderline flat.

It is very good for people who are very long waisted because it cuts the line; and it is also excellent for those of you who are big in the bust, because the fullness is very flattering.

If you are very petite, I would say avoid yokes, it is better for you to concentrate on frocks and coats with long lines and not ones that cut across you.

Young Look

Young Fashion. fect for youth—the rming white blouse b sailor collar and ize tie shown on e 123.

The young look is very nice on young people. But after a certain age it is better for you to concentrate on an elegant look rather than a young look.

There are certain things that are definitely for youth— Peter Pan collars ... tartan skirts ... quilted skirts ... pleats ... and some cotton materials. And there are certain things that are definitely *not* for the very young ... veils ... brocades ... black, gray and violet laces ... too much draping ... and a lot of feathers.

Zest

This is a happy word with which to end my dictionary of fashion.

Anything you do, work or pleasure, you have to do it with zest. You have to live with zest ... and that is the secret of beauty and fashion, too.

There is no beauty that is attractive without zest.

There is no fashion which is good without care, enthusiasm and zest behind it. Zest in designing ... zest in making ... and zest in wearing your clothes.

... Young ideas. Another sailor collar— this time on a short white evening dress.

Cover design: Andrew Prinz
Production Manager: Anet Sirna-Bruder

Cataloging-in-Publication data has been applied
for and is available from the Library of Congress.
ISBN: 978-0-8109-9461-4

First published by Cassell & Co. Ltd, 1954
This edition published by Abrams, 2007

Printed in Hong Kong
23 22

Abrams books are available at special discounts when purchased
in quantity for premiums and promotions as well as fundraising or
educational use. Special editions can also be created to specification.
For details, contact specialsales@abramsbooks.com or the
address below.

ABRAMS The Art of Books
195 Broadway, New York, NY 10007
abramsbooks.com